LEAN INTO ENTREPRENEURSHIP

How to Get Financial Freedom

Joyce Fiodembo

© 2019

DISCLAIMER

TABLE OF CONTENTS

BELIEVE

Do you believe you can have a thriving business?

It all begins in your mind.

I'd like you to do a simple exercise.

Take a moment, close your eyes, and dream about your business.

Visualize your business having plenty of employees, producing plenty of products, and making plenty of cash.

OK -now open your eyes.

Why do you think I began by making you do this exercise?

If you have any doubt about having a successful business, your doubt will become your reality.

I've done several businesses along my journey and the first step to make a business succeed is to visualize the success.

You don't have to be extremely business savvy, but rather, have the belief that your business will succeed.

Once you believe you can do a particular business, the next step is to take action.

Don't worry about the right timing. There never is a right time.

Once you look at your options and feel you need to begin a business, then just take that step of faith and move on.

The more you take action, the more you will get new ideas for even more action in the right direction.

There is only one thing that gets in the way of action, and that is your limiting belief.

Your limiting belief will convince you that you cannot succeed.

That is when you need to do a lot of self-talk and resist those negative thoughts.

Have the Right Mindset

Your mindset is your most important tool.

Natalie Sisson in her book, 'The Suitcase Entrepreneur' states that, 'to succeed you need the right mindset'

She takes the challenge of traveling around the world and running her business in different countries. She attributes her success to her right mindset.

Having the right mindset means knowing what is important to you.

Many of us are influenced by what society tells us. The society has a way of dictating how we need to live and it makes us get into all sorts of debts.

But for you to have a successful business, you will need to do things a little different from what your culture or neighbors and friends expect.

You may need to forfeit a part of your income, so you have extra time to begin your business.

What your friends and family think becomes irrelevant when you are building your business.

Let me share a little about my current business.

When I decided to begin my blog in 2012, I remember sharing the idea with my friends.

"What's the point of a blog?" Was what they asked.

I began to experience self-doubt. This made me nearly give up the idea.

I'm glad I did not listen to them because that original blog has opened many business ideas and opportunities for me.

If your thoughts are filled with doubt, your actions will follow what your subconscious mind dictates.

One way to get your mind in alignment with what you want to do is to have affirmations which you say daily.

What you say to yourself is more powerful than what others say to you.

Words

Words work in two ways - to build or destroy

What kind of words come out of your mouth?

Most people tend to repeat negative words and statements concerning the situations and events in their lives.

The way you use words determines whether they are going to bring you positive or negative results.

Do you say; 'I will succeed no matter what!' Or do you say, 'I wonder if I'll ever succeed?'

Your subconscious mind accepts as true what you keep saying.

It attracts corresponding events and situations into your life.

So choose to speak positive words to get positive results!

Using positive words begins with what you name your business.

Give your business a positive outlook. Don't let it appear boring or stiff.

People like things that energize them.

Let your business have an energizing and positive brand.

WHY THIS BUSINESS?

The best business for you to start is the one in which you have the greatest conviction and talent.

Your choice should not be influenced by your friends or any commercial advertisement. If you are like me, you may have a lot of different interests, and you are probably good at a lot of different things.

This means you can make money doing just about anything.

But the big question is; what business is best for you today?

What do you enjoy doing? And can you turn what you enjoy into a business?

These two are the most important questions for any aspiring new business owner when trying to decide what business is best for them.

There are five other things to consider before answering these two questions:

1. What would you be proud of doing?

Feeling good and proud of your business is necessary for you to succeed.

What means so much to you that you want to share it with your friends and neighbors?

2. What are you willing to continue learning about for as long as you are in business?

Business is like going on a long journey. On this journey, there are new things you will learn every day.

3. What type of customers do you enjoy working with?

No matter what business you start, put yourself in the role of customer service and support. Do not begin a baby-care business if you don't like the sound of crying babies.

4. What kind of people would you love to help over and over again?

To what degree do you want to work with them?

Quite often in business, the work becomes hard and draining. There are days you'll have to find within yourself a way to continue, even when you don't want to.

5. What do you believe in enough to want it for others more than for yourself?

Are you willing to train others in your skill?

Are you willing to become a mentor to others?

If your business idea aligns with the right answers, then you have tons of advantages.

Your learning curve won't be as steep, you can rely upon skills and knowledge that you've already built, and when things get tough, your passion will lead you to resilience.

If you have trouble deciding what your passion is, ask yourself the questions:

What business is best for you? -And what do you enjoy doing?

What Tools do You Need?

Evaluate your skills.

Your skills will be the foundation for having a successful business.

Evaluate your strengths and weaknesses.

For example, you may have an artistic nature or have good communicating skills.

After assessing yourself, ask; 'with these skills, what type of business can I start? '

Don't restrict yourself to a few skills. Make a list of all your skills at this juncture.

Test Your Business Idea

From this list of questions, strike off those ideas which are difficult or not possible, considering the resources you have access to.

For example, starting a manufacturing unit in a residential area is not the perfect idea. Be realistic and wise.

Expected Revenue

Before you begin any business,-consider your expected revenue and prepare a business plan.

Take these factors into consideration.

You may be very talented, but if you are not able to sell your product or services, your business will not succeed.

You have to access whether people are prepared to pay for your product or service so you can make a profit.

What is your Motive of Starting a Business?

Is it a side hustle to add to your income, or is it your full-time income?

Your motive will determine the amount of time you put into your start-up.

Prepare a Business Plan

When you put your idea on paper, you will be able to spot weaknesses and give you an opportunity to address them.

A business plan will help you gain clarity and keep you in touch with your vision.

You may need to write and re-write it several times. The good thing is that it does not cost you anything.

Spend more time on this in the beginning to ensure you manage your business better.

It is an Exciting Opportunity

Starting a business can be very challenging. But if you want to become your own boss and create jobs for others, it is an exciting opportunity.

Identify what you can excel in. The business environment is competitive, and finding a good opportunity may be difficult.

Success involves studying the trends in the business industry.

Analyze the demands for certain products and the income potential.

Be motivated and hardworking and be prepared to face the challenges.

Always be positive and make use of any help you can get.

Success Leaves Clues –Always

Look up to those individuals who are successful. Study them closely. Listen to what they say. Emulate what they do. They always leave several clues.

BUSINESS TOOLS

Once you determine what you want to transact as a business, you need to focus on the essential tools to get you started.

Do you want to sell cars, start a writing business, run a retail store or make websites for clients?

The next question you need to establish is, are you going to begin alone or do you plan to have partners?

Starting a business is not that difficult.

That considered, the setup rules vary from country to country.

So when it comes to regulations, you want to follow your country or state's legal procedures.

You want to establish what works and what doesn't work where you are.

Let's look at seven essential tools you will need.

1. Determine Your Start-up Cost

What are the initial costs to set up your business?

How many of each item do you need?

What is the initial number of staff required? What is the budget for salaries?

Do you need to rent business premises?

What do the utility bills cost?

2. Use Your Savings

Avoid borrowing too much money in the beginning.

You would not want to be saddled with debt, and you need a free mind to establish your business.

Knowing your startup costs means you can have a savings plan towards that end.

3. Choose Your Business Name

A business name is a name under which your entity will conduct business.

It is your business' identifier.

All businesses are required to have unique names.

Before you choose a name, ensure it does not belong to someone else and is not trademarked.

Otherwise, you will be served with an expensive lawsuit, and that's a terrible way to begin.

When choosing a business name, make it memorable. Let it represent what you are doing.

Some good examples are; Nike, Microsoft and Starbucks Coffee.

Never copy or modify renowned brand names.

For example; Amazonian. You will get into big trouble.

Get your original name.

Choose a business name that is easy to remember.

My friend's company is called 'Auriculares,' it means earphones in Spanish.

I can never remember or spell that name right. I have to jog my mind. I'm sure others are in the same boat as me.

If you have a business and your potential clients cannot spell it, you will lose customers.

Take your time and discuss your business name with your friends and colleagues.

Some professionals can help you come up with a name.

4. Register Your Business

Register the company according to your government regulations and standards.

Do you need insurance? If so, what kind of insurance?

What does it cost?

Ensure you have all the details.

Registering a business gives you several benefits.

It makes the company official and gives it legal standing. You can now legally offer services.

The government legally protects business owners.

To legally operate your business, you may be required to have certain permits and licenses.

These are country or state specific.

Be diligent and follow through.

5. Get Business Cards

These never go out of fashion. They are a small marketing tool you can give away anytime.

Those who say they are not necessary are poor marketers.

Good marketing means, do whatever you can to promote your business.

After you make connections with people, they want your address, phone, and contact.

You cannot write it on a piece of paper, no one will take you seriously if you do.

Business cards help you introduce your company to potential clients in a professional manner.

You can easily design your cards on your computer, or approach a designer or card company to make them for you.

6. Bank Account

Now that you have a business, you should open a business bank account.

A separate account from your other personal account allows for clean and accurate bookkeeping.

It demonstrates professionalism and is a legal requirement in some instances.

This may also have an impact on your tax returns.

Bear in mind that your business is an entity of its own.

7. Accounting tools

You can simply begin by using spreadsheets to maintain your data.

Alternatively, you can use free online software for your invoicing and simple accounting as your company grows.

Avoid expensive accounting tools and processes in the beginning.

You want to cut costs as much as possible.

Make sure you maintain proper accounting records for tax purposes and business growth.

Accounting is critical because poor accounting will break your business.

There are other tools you will need as your business progresses; however, these are essential at the start.

THREE INGREDIENTS YOU NEED

For you to call yourself a business person, your business needs three ingredients.

You need to have a product, you need to market it, and you need to look at the financial aspect to see if you are making sales.

If any of these are missing, then you are not in business.

Let's take a closer look at each. We will revisit them again later in detail.

A Product

To have a successful business, you need a product or service.

The gist of any business is that you have something to offer or sell.

It has to be something your prospects or clients want or need, or it can improve their lives one way or another.

Assume your writing skill is your product. What would you consider unique about your craft?

Are you a creative writer, good at keeping deadlines, meeting the client's needs and beyond?

Your product has to have a selling point that makes it stick out from the rest.

A good product will attract a clientele of its own accord.

People will be able to identify with your product. It should meet a need or a challenge they have been dealing with.

Business is a service. A good businessman solves a problem.

Look at Mark Zuckerberg, what problem does he solve? Or Jeff Bezos. Think of them as examples.

Even if your venture is small, let it solve a problem.

During the winter months, African hair gets so dry that if not well oiled, it breaks and falls.

A friend of mine noticed many of us were struggling to keep our hair moist.

She came up with Coco-Butter hair oil that is excellent for African hair texture. You bet her product sells like hotcakes.

I cannot overemphasize that you must let your product solve a problem.

Let it be easy to explain when someone asks you what you sell.

If you have to labor to explain your product, then you may have a problem.

A twelve-year-old should understand your product. If not, you need to get back to the drawing board and make your product easy to understand.

Marketing

Many people dread marketing.

The misconception has been that marketing is mean and to some extent evil.

Marketing has been vilified for a very long time because of the way some salespeople love to shove products down the prospect's throat.

This pushy style worked for a while, but with technology today, people have evolved to resist such methods.

Nowadays, people prefer to make their decisions. No one likes to feel manipulated into a decision.

It may make them hate your product.

That said, when you have a product, you need to sell it.

Marketing can best achieve this by informing the customers of the new product and its benefits.

Marketing is the lifeblood of your business.

Good marketing will educate your clients on the nature of your product and how it can benefit them.

Through marketing, you expand the reach of your services.

The ideal form of marketing is where you build a relationship with your client.

It could be using a blog post, videos, email marketing, or podcasting.

Once satisfied, the client then reaches out for your product of their free will.

This way, the client is appeased and later becomes your unemployed sales person, spreading the good news about your product.

Finances

In as much as it's hard to find an individual that shuns away from money, the idea of managing finances gives most people queasy knees. However, you cannot expect any form of success with your business without proper financial management.

At the very least, try to acquire some basic skills.

Finances are the backbone of your business. Without finance, you shall have no business to talk off.

You will not be able to fund the production of the commodity you sell.

Without money, it can be a challenge to run your marketing campaigns.

Not all things involving marketing call for money, however, not having it could profoundly hamper your capacity to deliver on commitments.

If you are weak at handling finances, recognize this and outsource this aspect of your business.

All Three Ingredients

It is impossible for one person to have all three ingredients.

Some people dream of finances daily. Others enjoy marketing, and someone has to make the product or offer the service.

Hire the services of other skilled people in what you lack, to help you handle the areas you are challenged with; and together you will keep the sailboat afloat preventing it from drifting to sea or sinking.

You need to know what you are good at and get help where you are weak.

All successful business people know and practice this principle.

That allows you to focus on what you do best.

It takes a team to do a successful business.

In the beginning, you will find yourself handling all three aspects while you are a startup.

But once you get rolling, you need to know what you are good at and outsource the other areas.

As your business grows, outsourcing becomes even more crucial.

YOUR TEAM

After completing high school, I got a job at a restaurant as a waiter.

This restaurant only opened between 11:00 am and 8:00 pm, and mainly served lunch and dinner.

The owner of the restaurant insisted on directly supervising the staff.

Unfortunately, he had the worst temper ever.

If his employees delayed with an order, he would yell so loudly at them.

In spite of the delicious food we served, and beautiful location and somewhat decent pay, many employees quit.

After two years, he closed down his business, incurring several losses.

Work Well with People

As your business grows, you need to work with a team.

Learn to work well with others and hire people who will be loyal to you.

The moment you suspect a lack of loyalty, it's time to fire them politely.

Your team can make or break you.

If your employee looks down on you or does not have any interest in your business, you will never excel in the area they are responsible for.

The people you hire must be self-motivated and be willing to go the extra mile.

Your business is as good as the people you hire!

Your business needs a team because you cannot do it all by yourself.

The challenge comes when we want to attract and hire top talent, particularly for startups, since you don't have a huge budget to work with.

You know that you need the best workers if you are to succeed in your business.

Beginning with yourself is important.

Do a Self-Assessment.

What are you good at doing?

If you need training, you should invest in yourself first.

Identify the skills your company needs.

Once you hire your team or employees, you want to retain them.

If you are good at marketing, then hire people who are great at product development or customer service.

Share Your Vision

For you to recruit the best talent, you need to be able to share your vision.

Have a passion for your business and let your team know you believe in your product.

Give your team the facts as to why you are going for that particular market as opposed to any other.

A young company has many surprises and there's lots of trial and error.

You will face many bumps along the journey.

Explain things to your team so that they are in the loop.

Inspire Your Employees

People with successful businesses are exceptional leaders who influence others to do their best.

Avoid bossing around or manipulating your employees.

Nobody expects you to be perfect, but they expect kindness, goodness, and fairness.

As the leader of your company, motivate and inspire your team.

If you are a good leader, your business will grow by leaps and bounds.

If your workers enjoy coming to work, they will do a great job.

Create a Strong Culture

Create a positive culture for the people you will work with.

Write down what is important to your company and share it with your employees.

Whatever values you choose, make sure you design your hiring process to make sure only people who believe in the same values get hired.

All your staff ought to believe in those values, even though they come from varied backgrounds.

Recruit people who are better than you in areas where you are weak.

Diversify your employees' economic backgrounds, education, and work experience.

It is diversity that will lead people to a broader range of potential solutions, which leads to better decisions, and results.

Strive to be an Effective Leader

Effective leaders put their employees in the best place to thrive and succeed.

They mix and match team members to make a well-rounded team that suits the organization -so that it runs smoothly.

As the leader of your business, your employees must trust you.

When you say something, mean what you say and say what you mean.

Be credible.

Your employees or contractors look up to you.

I remember doing a job for someone who promised to pay me $ 50. Then he paid me $

15 and said there were too many contractors and so he had to spread out his money.

Imagine how frustrated and disappointed I felt.

If you've had this experience, you'll never trust such an employer, and you'll probably spread the word to warn others.

Become a team player with your employees and support them in their growth.

Value them and let them know that you do, and they will do their best for your company.

Learn When to Say No!

As a leader of your business, you will get several requests from your employees.

You may not be able to fulfill all of them. So, it becomes crucial just to say No.

'When in doubt, say no.'

Most people avoid telling their employees the truth because it is uncomfortable.

You don't want to hurt people's feelings, and you are afraid of being judged.

But you know you cannot say yes to every request you get.

Tell your truth in love because it will set you free.

Be a Servant Leader

Robin Sharma, one of the top world business trainers, says your life has two purposes.

He speaks from the business perspective, not a religious standpoint.

Your purpose as a business person is to ask yourself; 'What are you becoming as you progress in your business?'

'And who are you helping on your journey?'

Your purpose is to serve humanity by the business you offer.

Remember to be a servant leader as you work with your team.

Times Have Changed

The old style of control, manipulation, and intimidation are ineffective these days, particularly in business.

Making statements like, 'if you don't deliver you're fired!' -are long gone.

Today, if you want productivity, you have to value your workers.

As the leader of your business, you need to motivate and inspire your team.

Work closely with your weak team members to see if they can improve before you decide to let them go.

When you value your workers, they will become creative, use their imagination and have faith in your company.

Succeed in your business by inspiring your team to perform at their best.

OVERCOME THE FEAR OF SELLING

There are lots of guides and articles that teach you how to overcome the fear of selling.

They even educate and show you strategies and tactics for solving the problem.

Read them.

You will collect an idea or two you can use to conquer your fear.

But if you want to end the fear of selling, you'll need expert advice from a person who has overcome the challenge.

In other words, advice from a person who has done it before, which is better than run-of-the-mill advice.

How do you do that?

Let's get started.

Fear of Rejection

Guess what?

People fear hearing rejection. The word 'no' is enough to end someone's career or even thwart their ambitions.

I used to fear rejection from people.

I would go as far as not bothering to pitch for my business in case I got rejected.

I later learned that if I hoped to get anywhere in my business, I would have to get comfortable with rejection.

Solution

Get comfortable with rejection when you are making a sale. Anytime a person tells you 'No, I am not interested, you have to ask the question; why aren't they interested?

Remember the person is not saying no to you. He or she is saying no to the product. You will get lots of answers if you ask that.

Another approach is to ask, 'Why do you feel that way?

Listen to how the buyer phrases their answer. You will learn a lot from the answer -and improve your sales game.

Fear of Delivery

I've experienced this fear many times in my career as an internet marketer. The internet is full of experts who know more than I do.

Even after the client says yes to me, -I still worry about living up to their expectation.

A point reached where I would suffer from 'impostor syndrome.' Then I started questioning the value of my services and products.

Solution

To solve this challenge, I did three things:

- First. After every project, I asked the client for feedback about my work. The feedback encouraged me a lot, realizing that I did everything they wanted.

- Second. I sought out ways I could improve my services to provide more value to my clients. I could read books, take courses, find a new tactic or strategy to make sure I am delivering the best for them.
- Third. Before I submitted each project, I wrote down the list of things I had done to make sure the client got more value from me than what they paid for.

Fear of Inadequacy

The number one reason most people fear selling is they don't know the sales process or their product very well.

Lack of education in sales and product knowledge makes lots of newbies afraid of sales. The moment your fear is bigger than your skills, you will chicken out of every opportunity. Your skills need to be bigger than your fear.

Solution

Before becoming an internet marketer, I sold a lot of jewelry for a company.

During that time, the organization emphasized on self and professional development. I used to read lots of sales book including, 'The Magic of Thinking Big,' 'How to Win Friends and Influence People,' and 'The Greatest Salesman In the World.'

Not only did my sales skills improve, but I also sold more jewelry during that time.

Read every book you know about sales, watch videos on YouTube, and attend more seminars. That way, you will increase your knowledge, and the fear will dissipate.

Fear of Sounding like a Used Car Salesman

No one hates being labeled a used car salesman as much as I do. It took long for me to change my thoughts on how I regard sales. I came to realize, selling is helping people and not selling the product.

If you have a great product, then you need to educate your customers on how that product will benefit them.

Solution

First. You have to understand the product or service you are offering. Second. You need to operate with the assumption you are helping clients benefit from your product.

Act as a consultant. A consultant will first identify your needs and ask lots of questions before they can even offer a solution.

The difference between a used car salesman and consultant is a used car salesman uses a pitch to sell you the product.

A consultant starts with a fact-finding question, to identify your needs, goals, and desires before asking you to buy.

Here is a set of questions a salesman wearing a hat of a qualified consultant will ask:

Have you ever used this product before?

What did you like about this product?

What was your experience?

How much did it cost you?

What three things would you want a new product or service to help you achieve?

That's how a consultant works. They will first ask you a question and then educate you on how their product can help you achieve your goals.

Let's face it!

Overcoming the fear of selling is not that easy. It's something you need to embrace and find a solution. Fear does one thing; it stops a person from doing something.

The best way to cure fear is to feed it with action.

Read more books, watch sales videos, and attend seminars. All these strategies have helped me improve my sales game and confidence.

Anytime I feel like I am afraid, -I refer to these tactics.

A CLOSER LOOK AT FINANCES

One of the reasons you started a business was probably to replace the income from your full-time job. Or maybe you were unemployed, and you realized you needed to survive; so naturally, starting a business was the best path for you.

I know several people who are extremely busy in their business, but the numbers do not add up.

Saying you own a business is much more than finding yourself busy.

The numbers in your bank account have to add up to something you can live off from. Let's look at how you can know your business profits.

Gross Income

For an employee, the whole of your contractual salary is considered your gross income. Assuming your salary is $3,500, and yet the paycheck handed to you is $2,500, the initial figure is deemed to be gross income. For a person with private business, all the revenue earned from whatever source, counts.

Say you are a freelance Life Coach, maybe you have invested in government bonds or the stock market, and are renting your property; all these incomes combined, add up to make your gross figure.

For businesses on the other hand, when it comes to gross income, what counts is the total money that the company generates before paying taxes, salaries or wages, or any expense.

It is from this amount that taxable income is computed. It consolidates profit realized in any form, be it money from services or property.

Net Income

The sum of money left of your salary after official deductions like taxes, retirement benefits, etcetera, is your Net Income.

Employing the above example, your salary is $3,500; after deductions, what is left is $2,500. That is your Net Income.

In the case of businesses, it is the money the company is left with after paying business expenses like rent, bank loan deposit, salaries, taxes, and etcetera.

How does it work?

Net Income = Gross Income - Total Expenses

Why does it matter?

Well, because a gross income offer is not necessarily what you will get in the end. The net is the total of what you are confident will end up in your pocket.

Cash Flow

It is a tricky aspect to appreciate. However, in a nutshell, it refers to the flow of real or virtual money. It has no relationship with how much money you have on hand or in the bank.

Cash flow accounts for the income realized minus payment of costs. Results from either money earned through investments or capital borrowed, generation of revenue from the selling of goods and services.

The cash flow can either be positive or negative. Positive cash flow means more money is coming in than that flowing out. Suggesting you can manage your business with no financial glitches as you can source the necessary funding, be it borrowed or from your vested earnings.

Negative cash flow, on the other hand, is more money going out -than is coming in. This implies you shall hit a financing hurdle at some point and be unable to conduct your business even though you technically have the money. Your money could be with debtors or held up somewhere, or payments are not yet due.

Cash flow is of much significance because it is one of the biggest reasons why startups fail -and big businesses collapse. Negative cash flow happens when your business operational costs are higher than the money it can raise.

Overhead Expenses

These are the fixed expenses or indirect costs of running a business. These could range from marketing costs and rent, to administrative costs.

Overhead refers to the expenses directly required to operate your business. Costs include accounting fees, insurance, legal fees, and advertising among others. Not covering direct labor or third-party expenses billed directly to customers.

Banking

The activity or industry of safeguarding and accepting other people's money by organizations is banking. The institutions may, in turn, lend out this money for a profit.

A bank is a financial establishment that is licensed and authorized by a government to accept deposits and act as an intermediary of financial transactions and make loans.

Other financial services banks offer include, -but are not limited to, currency exchange, wealth management, and safe deposit boxes. There are two types of banks: investment banks and retail or commercial banks.

Saving

According to the Business Dictionary, saving is the portion of disposable income not spent on consumption of consumer goods but accumulated or invested directly in capital equipment or in paying off a home mortgage, or indirectly through the purchase of securities. It is quite a mouthful.

You could say savings are the amount that is left over from a person's earnings or disposable income after expenses and cost of living are subtracted. That unspent income is derived from income minus consumption.

The portion of income deliberately not spent on current expenditure or intentionally set aside for a rainy day, is also considered a saving.

It is usually saved to cater for emergencies or unexpected events; the breakdown of your car, medical emergencies, and things like the purchase of a property.

YOUR CUSTOMER

In the business world, it may seem proper for the provider of services or goods to be the one continually passing communication to their clients.

After all, shouldn't they promote the product and persuade the client to purchase it?

While it may seem like the 'right thing to do,' it may make a prospective client lose interest.

Listening to your client is essential in business.

Let me share some of the reasons why you should listen to your client.

Product or Service Improvement

You may have conducted tests and concluded that your product provides excellent functionality and that your service is guaranteed to offer maximum satisfaction.

However, the end user is the customer, and their experience may reveal areas that need to be worked on further.

Having this information will enable you to go back to the design of the product or delivery of services and improve the weak areas.

When a client says they will not renew their subscription or that they would like to return your product, don't leave it at that. Get the reason why they would not make a repeat purchase and ask for their feedback in the areas that need improvement.

Offer clients value for their money, but also let them know that their feedback is valued.

Your clients will be pleased and come back as return customers knowing that they have been heard, and their expectations met.

Customer Retention

As a Business owner, -when you bring a product to the market, know that the customer is King.

Customers know what they want -and they also know they have a variety of choices at their disposal.

In competitive markets, the company which listens to its customers and acts on their requests is the one that can survive and thrive.

Therefore, listen to your clients; keep your communication lines open, and be open to embracing the changes that are required to improve their experience and retain them.

The cost of adapting to their requirements will be worth it.

An example of a company which did not listen to the clients' changing needs is Kodak.

Kodak was a big brand in the early 90s. However, clients generally moved to digital cameras -and Kodak took a while to catch up with the changes, hence they lost a lot of business and closed shop in several areas.

Valuable Information

Customers can give you useful information that is necessary for decision making.

There are bits of information which are not available from any other sources except your customers.

They will be able to tell you their experience should they have switched to purchasing from a competitor.

This enables you to know what they are doing differently. Customers can give you direct feedback on your products and can also study the trends in the market and inform you of a problem that can be predicted or will arise in the near future.

Qualitative information can also be sourced from clients. They will be able to inform you about how well you are meeting their needs compared to their ideal product or service.

The perceptions created when you re-brand can also be sourced from your clients.

The data sourced will give you useful information, and you can make a conclusion or draw up recommendations for what should be done so that the company succeeds.

Life of Your Business

A business exists to meet the needs of its clients with the aim of making a profit.

Besides knowing the product or service, the business person ought to know their customer.

By knowing them, they will understand their needs and be able to meet and exceed their expectations. Customer knowledge is vital for a business to succeed. Listen to your client to know their tastes and preferences as well as their valuable feedback.

When you focus on your customer, you are able to improve your business and have steady growth and reap profits.

In the business world, a company's life may end when it fails to listen to its clients.

Clients are the driving force behind the business and to succeed, you ought to take heed of their needs.

Business success is linked to customer centrality. Customers will make or break you.

Clients do have a say; after all, they pay for your product or service.

If you want your business to grow, then be silent at times and listen to the customer.

Make your Customers Love You

Listening to your customers does not cost you much, but it is guaranteed to grow your business. Not paying attention to your clients will cost you as they will feel like they are not valued and can opt to leave you for a competitor.

Go out of your way to please your customer. Show them you love and care about them. This way they will love you in return.

Not only should you listen but aim to understand the message they are conveying -and also act on the areas that need improvement.

Listening pays well; you will acknowledge this when your business succeeds.

SOCIAL MEDIA MARKETING

Technology has turned the world into a global village. The entry of social media made it even easier for people to connect- be it personal such as with family and friends in different ends of the world, or for business purposes, where a company uses social media to communicate to its audience.

Use social media to market your business.

Businesses that have not tapped into the opportunity availed by social media will lose out on sales.

Why Social Media?

Mobile usage in this day and age has increased. Most people go through their emails and social media accounts as soon as they wake up.

Social media offers you an inexpensive mode of marketing. It offers you a broad audience. Anything you post could end up on millions of people's screens. Also, you have the option to include creative images or videos to capture the attention of your audience.

The best way to use social media for business is to make it an open two-way communication channel. Social media offers customers a chance to be heard; therefore, you can offer an interactive platform to respond to your customer as soon as possible, and should any problem arise, you can act on it immediately.

Businesses use various best practices while handling social media. These include scheduling posts that will effectively reach the target market.

-Do some research on how to get maximum interaction and reaction from your posts across different social media platforms.

Some platforms, like Twitter and Facebook, may require you to post several times a day to get the message to your audience.

Sponsored posts or ads enable you to boost your online activity and have the message reach your intended audience. You can specify your target and narrow your advertisements to them.

Strategize

Social media marketing, just like any other aspect of a business, ought to have a strategy to achieve the desired result.

You are building a relationship with your online network. Personalize your online activity and be interactive. Be as human as you possibly can in your interactions.

Do not let your online audience feel as if they are communicating with an internet bot.

Just like other marketing activities, you ought to know your customer and communicate with them in the best way.

Consistency

You should portray a consistent brand image across the various platforms on which you engage with your customers. The messages passed should also be consistent and portray the image of your brand. You may use similar taglines, slogans, and logos across the various social media accounts for your business.

No More Teams

Selling before the introduction of the internet was a challenge. It would involve having a sales team, commonly referred to as foot soldiers, making cold calls and trying all methods to close a sale in one-on-one interactions. Technology has made it easier for you to sell; and everything, including increased sales, is just a click away.

If social media is used well to market your product or services, it can lead to increased sales. Recent researches done on demographics reflect that the decision makers are aged between 18 and 34 years old.

This group of people is also the largest user of social media. You can increase your sales by using the right social media platform in which your target market interacts.

Also, joining the groups where your potential customers are in gives you a better chance to make more sales.

The online audience is bombarded by all sorts of information when they log into social media. Therefore, you need to keep your posts short but sweet, -informative and engaging. Be responsive to any person who may express interest in what you are offering, and also provide details on how they can contact you.

Numbers Tell the Truth!

Words may not quite be convincing, but numbers never lie. To give you an estimate of the number of social media users who are potential leads and customers, here are some statistics on the number of active users on various social media platforms in 2018: These are the numbers carried on by Statista.com

Total Population using Social Media =3.03 Billion.

Facebook Users= 2.07 Billion a Month

YouTube= 1.8 Billion

Instagram = 800 Million

Twitter= 330 Million

Pinterest= 175 Million

LinkedIn =500 Million

Other platforms not mentioned like Tumblr, Meetup, etc. have several users.

With this overview, you can get a picture of how vital social media is for your business to thrive and survive.

Get Started

One of the best ways to get started is to create your profile page. This can be your personal page or a page set up specifically for your business.

Make sure the information is correct and that there are no typographic errors.

-The next step to growing your business is to do a search for the decision makers   in key industries and invite them into your network. Invite friends as well and begin to market your business.

Websites

Websites and blogs are a great way to market your business.

One link to your website regularly will spread the word and get people to know you well.

Update your website regularly, and keep posting updates on your social networking account.

Join forums of like-minded people to exchange ideas and concepts. Not only will you find people who will be interested in your business; you are also likely to meet prospective customers through this method.

If done well, social media marketing is a boom to business owners who can easily market their businesses online.

BRANDING YOUR BUSINESS

Let me start by asking you a question.

Is branding the same as marketing?

Jeff Bezos, founder of Amazon describes a brand as;

'Your brand is what people say about you when you're not in the room.'

This definition is correct because of the following two reasons:

First. Your brand comes from the experience your company delivers to your clients. This includes the product, services, company's value, pricing policy, and even small details like leaflets and websites.

Second. What matters the most is what people say about your organization. What do they say about your shareholders, employees, and your product?

Branding is not what you say about your organization. It is what people say.

It is evident what you do as a company or person will influence people's opinions.

In other words, it is the reason why you exist in the first place.

Let me share two fundamentals of building a perfect brand for your business.

Relevance and Specialization

A correlation exists between branding relevance and specialization.

The point being, you can't be relevant to every person. Your business has to be relevant to a select group of people. A focused business person will maintain relevance in the marketplace among customers who matter most.

Picture this example:

Dan makes high-end guitars for seasoned bluegrass musicians who want a specific, classic Martin-like cord.

Right off the gate, Dan's brand is not for persons who don't play guitar. It's also not relevant for many guitar players, pop stars or smash-grass musicians. Not even for classical guitarists.

Dan's brand of guitar appeals to bluegrass musicians. Does Dan worry about competition?

No. Dan's guitar brand is relevant to a small niche market. Rather than going for a wider net and pleasing everyone else, Dan appeals to one niche.

Second Example:

Do you remember the Blackberry?

The blackberry phone was typical among the young, hyper-busy professional. The product is not relevant today. Technological advances from Apple and Google swept Blackberry off the market.

These two examples show two things:

Relevance equates to meaningfulness. In other words, a meaningful brand generates interest and desire from people. Desire and interest move people to take action.

The main reason why brands fail is they didn't mean anything in the first place. Some brands lose their meaning over time.

Do you remember Motorola?

Some brands lose their market share because of credibility.

Credibility

Credibility creates the core essence of your brand.

Credibility starts in knowing yourself, your brand, and the essence of why a company exists.

You can never be true to yourself if you don't know why you exist and what you care about.

Take a paper and write down your purpose, your obsession, and your promise to the customers. All great brands have their value and principles -and they live it.

Branding is about keeping the promise you make to your customer. It's through this commitment that you build trust, credibility, and loyalty. Never confuse customers by preaching about what you can do or deliver, they won't buy it.

Salespeople often rant about the reality of over-delivering to get a sale from their customer. One thing you have to understand is, if you over-promise and you come up short, you lose credibility.

Set Realistic Expectations

It doesn't matter if you are a business or a person. Set realistic expectations for your customer. In case things go wrong, always admit you are wrong.

Suppose you are a strong brand and you know yourself. The best way to mess up is to market or advertise something your brand does not stand for.

Associate with the Right People

Don't be like a criminal lawyer who claims to be friendly and honest. If you want to get into a problem, try working with a celebrity of questionable character to promote your product or service. Every brand affiliate has an impact on your business.

Building a Brand Begins with a Simple Idea

The advertisement industry is full of ideas. Companies that start with a simple idea and stick to it, become iconic brands.

Maytag came up with the idea of worry-free kitchen appliances. Their advertising and marketing sticks to the idea of dependability and reliability.

In other words, no one else will claim to own the idea of reliability and dependability. Customers trust Maytag for that.

Google came up with the idea of search. It has grown so much that it is a verb; 'Google it.'

McDonald's took the idea of fast food.

Subway took another angle from McDonald's and they now own the idea of 'Healthy Fast Food' which is healthier than McDonald's.

It's no secret the idea made Subway the number one in the fast food category. Today they are more than 44,000 Subway stores compared to 36,000 McDonald's stores.

Coming up with a brand is difficult. The best way is to study existing businesses and understand their model.

Your Brand Message

Most importantly, have the right marketing message that will work to promote your product.

The best way to know if you have a branding strategy that works is by the number of sales you are getting.

The three most important questions you need to ask yourself are:

Are you getting the right customers who need your service or product?

Do they buy from you?

Do they come back to buy from you?

If you have a strong brand, it will move the sales needle. Before a customer decides what to buy, they will choose the best brands. Customers do that to avoid risks. Let's say your product is relevant and customers trust you, they will often buy from you.

Relationship Branding

You can have a brand and sell to a small group of friends who know you. For example, 'Homemade Honey.'

Selling based on personal relationship and low-price margin works well if you are a small business or have less competition. But your brand won't stay in the market for long. At some point, you have to scale up.

Stand Out From the Crowd!

Branding helps your company stand out.

There are probably many businesses offering similar services as you are.

What makes you different from the rest? Why should they choose you over others?

Proper branding will place you ahead of your competition.

Repeat business is the key. If a customer only buys from you once, something is wrong with your brand.

The quality of your service is what brings customers back. As we have said before, branding is what people say about your organization.

THE SMART WAY TO NETWORK

Networking is the process of building a relationship with people and other business establishments, with the purpose of having a base-which can be tapped into, to increase one's revenue and bring about a profit.

The way this works is that it allows you to have maximum visibility in the business world. It also builds extensive contacts which can be easily used to make a better business deal.

Starting any business first requires a customer base. What are you going to sell?

Every company sells something, be it a product or service.

Either way, you need the audience that will make your business a success. Targeting an audience and convincing them to be your client requires you to adhere to some essential networking tips.

A Life Skill

Networking is a fundamental business and life skill. It is the ongoing process of building and developing a web of mutually beneficial relationships. In other words, you meet people and build some kind of relationship with them, whether it's a deep friendship or occasional business contact.

You strengthen relationships by communicating with people, providing them with things they need, finding common interests, and doing things together.

The relationship is cemented when the other person finds a way to help you in the form of information, support, or business referrals.

As you repeat this process with more and more people, you will have an ever-expanding pool of contacts that you know, have done things for, and can count on for help. Relationships can grow stronger, fade away, and perhaps end. However, an experienced networker will have a net growth in their base of close friends, and the sheer number of people they have interacted with.

How to Network for Your Business

The rule of thumb for networking revolves around developing a trustworthy business relationship. Following up on referrals is important and delivering what you have promised will make sure that your networking endeavors are truly rewarded. Following are some tips to help you network successfully.

Know Your Business

You need to have a thorough understanding of what the goal of your business is so that when you meet people, you can explain it to them. Knowledge of your business also makes you more confident and enables people to have faith in you. Be prepared for all sorts of questions regarding the feasibility and other aspects of your business.

Be well versed because only then, will people know that you are a serious business person who has thought things through, and not someone who had a short business idea and is out to implement it without considering its potential.

Start with People You Know

Start by spreading the word among your peers, colleagues, and others who know you well.

These are the people who will spread the word for you. Involve those willing to join you so that your circle of influence expands and you can reach out to more people.

Go where your Customers Are

Recognize your potential customers and network, and make sure you are present wherever your audience is.

When you communicate with them, exude confidence and passion. Use language you know will engage the listener. When you introduce your business, speak of the concept behind, before you talk about what you do.

This will help you explain your business idea better and develop the necessary contacts to build your business. Even if you develop a few contacts, they are likely to be of great benefit to start with.

You Need a Strategy

Have a networking strategy. Who do you want to relate to and why? Men tend to be better than women because they get straight to the point. If it's a friendly get-together meeting, then go ahead and make several friends. But for a business person, this may be your only opportunity to meet certain people you want to connect with, -so don't waste time.

Go to them and introduce yourself. Tell them something pleasing, even if you have to say, 'I like your T-shirt.' -This will make them pay attention, and you can begin a conversation from that point.

Update Your Network

Provide updates on what you've been working on and the results. This will increase your reputation as an expert in your field and lead people to use you as a resource, and share with others in their networks. As your reputation grows, so will your network and you will find it easy to grow your business. Take a few minutes each day to build relationships. Expand your contacts with one person at a time.

In Conclusion

Make strong favorable first impressions.

Remember people's names even if it means you write them down immediately. Find value in people and share what value you have for them.

If you turn the foundation of networking into a simple process of building relationships -you'll find yourself owning a large business with not much effort.

IMPORTANCE OF MENTORSHIP

Whether you are looking to start a new business or you have an existing business, the fact remains; you need a mentor to challenge your thoughts and help you move the needle in your industry.

A mentor is a person who has done the same thing as you and has more experience than you in the chosen field.

But before I share with you the importance of a mentor, you need to understand why you need one mentor in your life.

Follow One Mentor

People often get confused and sidetracked by all the conflicting advice they receive.

They take lots of courses, listen to different experts, and try to bring all the advice together themselves and figure it out.

The reality is, if you did everything those people say, it would probably work. But you can't follow more than one mentor at a time -it's impossible. So, choose one person.

Listen to one mentor until you've implemented everything they suggest.

If you have enrolled in other courses, bow out of them. Stop following them, stop listening to them on YouTube.

And for God's sake, don't buy anything else!

Focus on what you have in front of you and do the work.

Let's look at the benefit of mentorship.

Gets You Out of your Comfort Zone

A good mentor will get you out of your comfort zone.

Friends and family will want to comfort you and help you stay small, but a mentor will encourage you.

Most important, they will make you improve and push you to realize new experiences.

The great thing about a mentor is they help you plan and thrive. If you get the right mentor, it will be an excellent reward, taking in new knowledge and advice.

A study from the Journal of applied psychology found that business people who were mentored experienced more business success than those who were not.

Sheryl Sandberg; in reference to this study states, 'both men and women with mentors are more likely to ask for raises.'

Show You Areas You Can Improve

It's so hard to know the areas you can improve on when your business is stagnant or when you are the best in the market.

A great mentor will come with an outside perspective and share with you areas in your business that need your attention, because they have a bird's eye view.

They will tell you the brutal truth rather than downplay on your weakness. In other words, they will see or spot things you could not recognize.

Business profits and yearly targets can blind you to think you are growing when you are not. A great mentor will not only improve the success of your business, but they will also double your profit and revenue.

Connect You to New Networks

Do you know that if you have an excellent working relationship with your mentor you can tap into his or her network?

Chances are, your mentor has a pool of networks and connections.

Let's say you want to go to China and supply your merchandise there.

If you open up your concerns with your mentor, they may help you get a partner who has connections in China that you had no idea about.

Share Constructive Criticism

Constructive criticism is vital because it helps you grow as an entrepreneur.

A good mentor will criticize you when you are about to make the wrong move. Any time a mentor criticizes you, don't take it personally. Use it as a catalyst to improve your character and your business.

I know how accepting criticism or advice is sometimes difficult. However, if you want to grow and become the best in your field, you have to accept criticism and use it to change your decision or your view.

Stimulate Personal and Professional Growth

A famous director once said 'the delicate balance of mentorship lies in allowing the person to create their image, but not creating the image for them.'

In other words, a mentor helps you become a better version of yourself.

Goal Setting

The main reasons why people fail in goal setting is, they don't have a mentor who can remind them of the promise they made.

A great mentor will watch you from a distance to see how your projects and goals progress.

They will then tell you what they have observed. For instance, it is easy to feel scared when making colossal business decisions responsible for your growth.

But it's the mentor that will push you and instill the values of discipline so you can grow.

Create Boundaries You Cannot Set for Yourself

Self-discipline doesn't come easily. Did you know it is so hard for you to set boundaries for yourself?

Being an entrepreneur is challenging because self-discipline is paramount. The good news is, a great mentor will take the role of a parent to make sure you are disciplined and set successful habits and principles to stick to, every day.

Anytime you fail or come short; they will call and remind you of the mission you have. Best of all, they will help you clarify and prioritize your life.

Finally

Great entrepreneurs like Elon Musk, Sir Richard Branson, or even Facebook's Mark Zuckerberg didn't become great by chance. Neither did they have superhuman abilities since their childhood.

What you may not realize is, they all had mentors who were behind the scenes. Great athletes have mentors too. In other words, if you want to prosper not just in business but in life, you need a mentor. They will cut your success curve and make you prosper both in your professional life, and in your business.

CONCLUSION

Now that you have all the tools to become a successful entrepreneur, I want to share five things I'd like you to remember.

You are special because when you succeed, you create jobs and change people's lives for the better.

Be Self Driven

Do whatever it takes to be self-driven. You may need to listen to motivational talks every day to keep you going.

If you like to be spoon fed, you'll not go far. You have to be disciplined enough to run your own show.

Be Creative

Imagine and try stuff out. Be a visionary and think Big.

Even if your idea seems outrageous to others, try it out in small proportions to see if it will fly.

Don't let fear and discouragement stop you from trying out stuff. Think about the founder of Amazon. When he shared the idea of everything being sold from a website, his peers laughed at him.

'Ha, ha, ha!' 'Who would shop from a website?' they asked. -Well, who's laughing now?

What if he had felt discouraged from all the laughter and had given up?

Have Perseverance

When the going gets tough, and it will, don't quit.

Business is not for the faint-hearted. Hang in there. Better days will come.

Focus on Creating Value

Create something that is useful to someone. Or sell something that solves a problem.

Business is about service. If all you want is profit that is a model that will not last. But if you are offering a service, then you will go far.

Collaborate with Others

I like the African proverb; 'If you travel alone, you go FAST if you travel with others you go FAR.'

It's never a one-person journey. You will get burned out, or you will not progress if you try to do everything by yourself.

You need others to walk with you. You need employees, mentors and support groups.

You need a team because as the saying goes; 'team work makes the dream work!'

Thank You!

Thank you for buying this book. I am honored by your decision.

I wish you all the best in your business.

Please take a moment to give me a positive review.

You are most welcome to visit my website at www.joyzeal.com

Blessings!

Joyce

www.ingramcontent.com/pod-product-compliance
Lightning Source LLC
Chambersburg PA
CBHW020926180526
45163CB00007B/2906